Photoshop
Master the Basics 2

*9 Techniques to Take Your
Photoshop Skills to the Next Level*

James Carren

For more books by this author, please visit
www.photographybooks.us

Table of Contents

Introduction

Welcome to the second installation of my book on Photoshop, or more specifically, the usage of the Photoshop found within Adobe Creative Cloud. Other recent versions of Photoshop will be similar as well, but try to stay fairly recent.

In the first edition on Photoshop, we discussed all of the basics: how to become familiarized with the workspace and set it up for optimization of your own per-sonal workflow, what tools are where, what they're meant for, and how to apply them. Once orientation was established, image preparation was discussed. Again, just in passing, I want to discuss how important it is to make sure that your image is properly prepared before going ahead with any type of editing or changes. As you know, that is the first building block to creating an image that will be the highest resolution. Initial file type influences all of this, so just be mindful from the beginning and you'll be off to a good start.

The other building block discussed in the previous book is layers. Layers prevent you from working right on top of your image, which means that if you need to, you can use the history tool to go back to the start. This tool also allows you to turn the layers off and on, which gives you the capability to see what you've done and whether or not it's working. Layers are going to be your best friend, so use them, and use them often. Always label everything you do in a clear, precise way so that you know what each layer refers to. Now that you've had a refresher on your image setup, let's move into what this book will cover.

- The Filter Gallery; where it is and why it's important. The Filter Gallery can be used for all sorts of things, from making editing that much easier, to making a photo look more natural, to fun and crazy fine art applications.

- Simple portrait edits; nothing fancy, this section includes information on things like how to remove redness from the skin, how to smooth wrinkles or large pores, and how to remove red eye and flyaway hairs. Basically, it's about taking your subject's natural attractiveness and making it stand out without it seeming like any corrections have been made.

- More advanced portrait retouching; this isn't for your everyday headshot or senior portrait. This chapter focuses on what you do when you have things like beauty or fashion shots. It starts out with the proper usage of the liquefy tool, which allows the user to reshape bodies and facial features as subtly or as dramatically as needed. There are also other techniques that I will mention that will give that high-end, airbrushed look.

- Moving on from portraiture, there is a chapter on colorization. Coloriza-tion is a throwback from the world of early photography, where photographers painted black and white photographs to appear to be full color. Today, the technique is much the same, except that it's much easier and mistakes can be more easily corrected with the aid of Photoshop. I will discuss how to colorize selected portions of an image, as well as the whole thing.

- Color enhancement simply refers to taking what you have in an existing color image and getting the most out of it. It involves making sure that colors and light levels are clean and appropriately vibrant, without being overly saturated. It's essentially basic retouching for a landscape or still life photograph.

- Background removal is a lot simpler than you might think. It's also a useful skill to have, especially as it relates to the world of product photography and of collage.

- Camera RAW of course gets its own chapter, because it is absolutely inte-gral to creating good photographs. If you are a budding professional, it is important to always shoot RAW and to get into the habit of doing at least preliminary developments within the Camera RAW dialog box. This will allow you to get the most out of your base image, and then you can apply other things such as filters and cool effects within Photoshop's main program.

- HDR is high-definition imaging, which involves combining multiple exposures to get the best overall exposure of the scene. The images are crisp and almost surreal looking. Believe it or not, this process is incredibly simple to achieve.

- Smart objects allow you to render 3D elements within your image. I will explain what they are and how they work, as well as some photographic instances for using them. Finally, life will get much easier when you understand how to use the Batch Editing dialog to your advantage to help you manage your presets.

That being said, let's move into the first chapter, on the filter gallery.

Chapter 1
The Filter Gallery

The filter gallery can be found in the Photoshop navigation bar. It has its own place in every version of Photoshop. When you pull down the menu, you'll see a variety of choices. Of course, there is a selection that will allow you to apply your last filter used and all its settings to the next photograph you're working on. I have found that this option doesn't really work for me unless the settings of all the photos I'm working on are nearly the same.

When you click on the main filter gallery, it's going to bring up a dialog box of all the filters that can be used, and the one you've used most recently is automatically going to be up on the screen. I like to go straight into the whole filter gallery when I'm experimenting, layering, or not sure exactly which effect I'm looking for. Alternatively, there are some other commonly used filters that are mainly used as fixes or with other processes, and these are categorized into submenus. If you go into the submenu, another dropdown listing the filters comes up. Some of them can require some testing, but most are pretty self-explanatory. If you are unsure about any selection, though, don't worry. Whether you choose to go into the Filter Gallery in its entirety or to use the dropdown menus, a dialog box is going to pop up that will allow you to see your current image in a window, so that as you adjust any sliders, you can see the changes you're making before they are applied.

In the main gallery, everything is grouped under a category heading to make things easier. You will see things like: Artistic, Brush Strokes, Distort, Sketch, Stylize, and Texture. Some categories have more filters than others, and Pho-toshop always comes with a preset amount of filters, although as you advance in your skills, you may choose to download more from other sources and place them in your gallery.

Even though each filter is represented with a small thumbnail, if you have the time, I really would suggest playing around with the dialog and applying a few to a test picture just to see what you can come up with. As with blend modes, the possibilities are nearly endless. Don't forget to play around with the provided sliders and see how that alters the effect, too.

Some filters, depending on their complexity and the intensity, can take a minute to load once you have applied them. This is fine, just be patient. In addition to certain lens fixes and other corrective things you can do, many fine artists use the filter gallery to completely alter the look and feel of their image. If you only use one filter, the effect can be quite obvious, but after several layers, it can be transformed to look like a painting, an etching, or a collage.

Underneath the main filter gallery is a filter called Adaptive Wide Angle, which is used to either correct or to add any lens distortion looks you might have or want. If you're unsure what a tool does in this dialog box, just place your mouse over the tool and Photoshop will help you out. Adaptive Wide Angle is mostly for adding that artsy, distorted flair. If you really have an aberration you can't stand, I would suggest using the Lens Correction Filter instead.

We will discuss Camera Raw and why I love it later in the book, but for now you should know that right underneath the Adaptive Wide Angle is the Camera Raw filter. This is particularly useful if you've got a RAW file and you've done your corrections, closed the dialog box, opened it up in the main Photoshop workspace, and then realized you did something wrong or that you weren't quite as done as you initially thought.

Now, I know we've already discussed the Adaptive Wide Angle filter, but there is also the Lens Correction filter, which is much more specific. Where with the Adaptive Wide Angle, you are choosing to add any lens distortion, here, it's all about correcting any mistakes or weird distortions your lens may have caused. This filter is a really good tool to use all the time, and I would even suggest running a Lens Correction filter on all of your final images after basic corrections have been done.

The way the Lens Correction works is very specific. Starting with the Auto Correction tab, you can select the camera make and model as well as the lens model you shot your image on. This helps the program to identify the common issues that that particular camera or lens may have and correct them. As you add lens profiles, Photoshop will save them so that you can just select the correct one from the dropdown menu later on.

Then you will move to the Custom Corrections tab, where you can correct such things as geometric distortion, chromatic aberration (also known as color fringes; some lenses, for example, are known to be slightly magenta or green, et cetera), add a vignette to your image (just don't, use the slider for good and use it to remove any vignette you might have) or correct perspective with transform tools.

Vanishing Point exists for correcting perspective. As always, before you begin in Vanishing Point, you should create a new layer for your changes to exist on. After you have created this layer, then open the Vanishing Point Dialog box. Working on top of a layer is also great because it means you can control the areas the perspective correction affects by utilizing layer masks. You'll also be able to preserve all other settings of your original image. You can also copy and paste images or parts of images in perspective, as long as you do the copying, and then the pasting within the dialog box for each image. So for example, if you want to copy something, open Vanishing Point, do your corrections, copy, close Vanishing Point, reopen it with your second image, and then paste. Corrections will be preserved. You can do the same with selections of parts of images.

So now let's talk about the functions of the tool itself. First, you will be asked to click the four corners of your plane in order to define where you'll be working. It's entirely possible that you will not be fully satisfied with your initial selection, and you'll need to make some adjustments. Using the Edit Plane Tool, you can reshape by dragging the corners, adjust the grid size to visually give boundary to the details you want it to, click and drag to move the plane around entirely, or scale the plane by dragging around your edge nodes within your boundaries.

If all of this sounds like a foreign language right now, I would suggest that you play around with it. We know intuitively how perspective works, so just use this tool as an adjustment to make sure that everything is lined up correctly.

In order to keep everything perfectly correct, it is very likely that you'll need to create overlapping planes, so what you'll do is tear off a new plane from an existing one. This is done by going to Edit Plane and Command dragging an edge node (not a corner node) of the bounding box. Voila! You've got a second plane, and if needed you can tear off from that one as well. Be sure to always adjust the angles of your planes accordingly within the dialog box. New planes automatically tear off at a 90 degree angle, but that's not always going to be sufficient. If you are unsure of your angle, just get it in the ballpark and then play around with it until it looks right.

It's important to understand what it means when your grid changes color. If you've got a blue grid, it means you've got a proper plane. All this means is that all vanishing points of the grid can be resolved, although this does not guarantee that the perspective you've corrected the image to is correct. Remember that Photoshop is just a tool, and that it still requires you to pay attention that the grid, which is your guide, lines up with the existing elements. Red means the plane is invalid, and yellow means that parts of the plane are invalid. It is possible to work from an invalid plane, but your results will get wonky. I could see where the perspective tool could be valuable within conceptual fine art, to completely create images that defy the laws of perspective, but I think it's important to learn to use the tool for its intended use first before going that far.

Keep in mind that you definitely want to utilize selections and cloning, stamping, moving, rotating, and scaling within Vanishing Point. That way, once perspective is correct within the image, you can make sure that all elements, such as windows, doors, and details, are all in their proper place. Alternatively, you can fill selections (doors, windows, et cetera) if you don't want them to be there. Although achieving perfect perspective brings an image closer to visual reality, you might want to use these tools to maintain flow or aesthetic within the image. Everything is always up to your aesthetic choice. I would suggest this filter most for things like wide-angle landscape, pictures of interiors, or very geometric abstract patterning.

Explore the Filters gallery in order to make your work look that much more creative, professional, and put together. Take the time to experiment with each, preferably on the same image so that you can see what all the different filters do.

Chapter 2
Simple Portrait Edits

Let's start out with some simple portrait edits. When I say simple portrait edits, what I'm referring to are the kind of fixes that don't look obvious, that retain the natural beauty or attractiveness of your subject. With these kinds of edits, you don't want someone (other than perhaps a professional) to be able to look at the image and know that anything's been done to it. Basically, you want to optimize how your subject already looks. Of course, you want to begin with a photo that is well exposed, sharp and beautifully composed. The kinds of things you want to fix are: making the skin naturally smooth looking, while still retaining tone and texture and attributes such as freckles, while removing acne, making deep wrinkles around the eyes, nose and mouth less harsh but still present, removing any skin redness or blotches, brightening and sharpening eyes and eyelashes, and maintaining texture in hair, lips, and eyebrows while making sure there are no stray hairs or dust.

Let's begin with acne removal, which also operates with redness removal.

Acne/Redness Removal

Let's start with the adjustment layer. You want to create a Hue/Saturation ad-justment layer which is going to allow you to not only work on a separate layer from your image, but is going to allow you to target only the red colors in the photo. This technique is also going to be the same basic starting place you would use as when you're trying to remove heat blotches or rosacea, or something similar.

In your new Hue/Saturation layer, go up to your Master dropdown menu and select the red channels. Push your Hue and Saturation sliders to their max. This is going to make your photo look very strange, but not to worry. It's just so that you can see what all the sliders are currently affecting and narrow that range so that your changes will only affect the areas you want them to.

Notice that down at the bottom is a double slider, which converts the color selected by the above slider into the color selected by the slider below. If you move that around a little bit, the image will begin to look more normal, and you'll be clearly able to see what colors are actually being affected. What you want to do is make sure that all the red or acne affected areas are highlighted by that other color. That's how you make Photoshop target those areas when you go to fix them. You want to narrow that area down as much as possible so that really only the acne reds are affected, as opposed to every red present in the photo. You'll know that you got it in the ballpark if your subject's lips are also slightly being affected.

Next, bring your hue and saturation back to normal, while leaving the bottom sliders where they are. Also bring up the lightness just a little bit. You should be able to see that your subject's face looks much less red than it did to begin with. If you have any areas of the photo that should be red, such as lips or hair or a wall, just go in with the brush on your layer mask and bring that color back in.

Now, we tackle the acne. This is where your spot healing brush tool comes in. Make sure you create a new layer on which you remove the acne, so that you aren't directly affecting your master image. Once you have that selected, zoom in on your picture to the area where the acne is. If you have a lot of acne, that's okay, you still want to zoom in so that you can be sure you're going to affect only the pixels you want and need to with your brush. Also be sure to be continually adjusting your brush size as you work; you don't want to be using a very large brush on a small area because you'll affect parts of the skin you didn't intend to.

Make sure that for this, the button at the top labeled Content Aware is selected. As Photoshop works to correct the blemishes you select, you want to be sure you've told it to pay attention to the content of your image. As you use your Spot Healing Brush, be sure to click on the parts you want to affect, as opposed to making the mistake of dragging to cover more ground faster. Not only is this lazy, but again, you will affect pixels that you didn't initially intend to. You might have to click several times to fully remove a blemish, but it will only remove in that area instead of incorrectly affecting your entire image.

Skin Smoothing

You always want to do redness removal and acne removal before moving on to skin smoothing. That way, you have nice, clean skin to work with. No matter the age of your subject, you will want to do some skin smoothing, although age and personal preference will really determine how much you do. For this step, you'll want to duplicate your background layer with all of the corrections you've applied thus far. At this point it may even be a good idea to consider grouping your corrections by folder so that you don't get confused or accidentally rearrange something and set yourself back.

So, duplicate the background image you would like to start with. Change the blend mode of the copy to overlay, and go to Filter>Other>High Pass. What the High Pass filter does is sharpen an image, so you're going to see a big increase in sharpness. You might be thinking, why in the world would I want to do that? But it's good because what it's going to serve to do is make sure that as you soften, you can also keep things like eyes, lips, and hair very sharp. When the High Pass dialog comes up, you're going to see what looks like a greyed out version of your image. What you want to do is increase the radius until you can see detail in the eyes and around the mouth. The radius will be different for every image, but I would say that somewhere around a 6 or 8 is good, but just be sure to watch your details, such as wrinkles around the eyes or mouth. When you hit OK, don't panic. Your image is going to look way too over-sharpened, which really is the antithesis of what we're trying to do. So now, hit command and I and invert the image. What you'll have instead is a very soft image, which is awesome for the skin, but not so great for things like eyes and hair.

To fix this and create the final image, you'll need to add a layer mask to the copy layer. Using your brush, brush through the parts of the image that need to be sharp. Also, allow some of the wrinkles around the eyes and mouth to come in.

Wrinkles

While the above technique should do well to take care of minimal wrinkles or to make wrinkles less noticeable without completely getting rid of them, when you have deep wrinkles, you'll need to employ some other techniques. One is to use the Healing Brush. This is the sister tool to the Spot Healing tool, and can be used to cover large areas. As usual, you should create a new layer to work on before you begin. You also need to do some setup, and make sure that "sample all layers" is selected from the dropdown menu at the top. Also, make sure the checkbox labeled Aligned is unchecked. It makes it easier to work with all healing tools in general.

The next step is to find a good, smooth area of skin to sample. Unless you are working with a very old person, this shouldn't be too hard to do, but I would suggest keeping the areas you sample as close to the area of the wrinkle you're working with as possible, and I would also zoom in and find a small area. As you move around the face, make sure you sample a new area of skin. Don't try to use the same sample from around the eyes for an area around the mouth, for example. This will help make your image look the most natural. To sample, Photoshop will prompt you to hold down option and click.

If you're working with a relatively young person, you may be able to remove a wrinkle entirely or just to leave a tiny hint of it, and have your image still look natural. However, if the person is older and/or has deeper wrinkles and scars, you don't want to remove them entirely or the image will look odd. So, start with the smallest part of the wrinkle and work your way up. Make sure that your brush is approximately larger than the wrinkle at hand, but not by too much. You can easily use your bracket keys to make the brush smaller or larger as needed. You'll also want to sample different bits of skin as you move along to avoid making the photo look strange, like it has the same information repasted over and over into different areas. I have also never found working in large swathes to be very effective when it comes to the replacement quality. Plus, if you make a mistake, it's just that much more that you have to redo. Work in smaller strokes to conserve time and energy.

If you are working with someone who has very little wrinkles, you should be close to done at this point. However, if you are working with someone with a multitude of wrinkles, you'll want their face not to look quite so smooth, so lower the opacity of your corrections layer in order to make the effect look more natural.

Teeth and Eye Brightening

At this point, your image is probably looking pretty good, but there are a few other things you can do to add a bit more pop. Two of these are to brighten up the eyes and teeth. Luckily, both can be done with the same tool, the dodge tool. You might have to play around with it a bit, but odds are that both your teeth and whites of eyes are going to fall into the range of midtones. Make a whitening layer, and feel free to use the same one for both the teeth and eyes. Adjust the exposure up in the top bar to adjust how much you would like the area to be whitened. Start with around 30 or 40 percent, and crank it up from there if you need to. If you find that the dodge job is too white for your liking, simply go to the Edit toolbar and you will see an option called Fade Dodge Tool. Select this, and a dialog box will pop up, where you can adjust the percentage of fade.

Be careful as you are working on the eyes, so that you don't affect the color of the irises too much.

Flyaway Hair

Even though we want to keep our images as natural looking as possible for this section, it's always a little pesky when your photo looks perfect and then there are one or two hairs out of place.

Once again, you'll want to create a new layer. If I cannot impress anything else on you in this book, it will be how important layers are.

If you have a solid background behind your subject, this is going to be a fairly easy fix. Create a new layer, pick out the Clone Stamp Tool, get a soft brush that's large enough (but not too large) for the area you would like to cover, and paint over the hair. You're just bringing the background in to cover up the hair you don't want to see. If you've accidentally removed any hair you didn't want to, you can bring it back via use of a layer mask. Keep in mind that this fix will only work well with pictures or areas of pictures that have a solid background to sample from. One fix is to play around with the blend mode of the cover up, and see if something works. If it does, great! If not, it's time to add some blur. Specifically, you need to create a new layer and add on some surface blur. What you want to do is set your threshold at such a point that the tool will know (via change in color) when to stop the blur. Using the preview in the dialog box, watch the blur until it begins to affect areas you don't want it to. Keep it just below that point, and the tool will preserve large chunks of that color, (e.g. the hair), but not the smaller ones (the flyaways). Play around with the radius to see at what point it stops having a cleansing effect. You also don't want it too low or color will begin bleeding into the background, which isn't good.

This should get you fairly close to where you need to be, but keep in mind that you may have to create a second blur layer and run surface blur one more time to clean up some other parts. Just zoom in on the bits that still need some help, and clone stamp it out. Note: DO NOT try to do this if you aren't zoomed way into the area where you're working. Zooming will also help if your background has got some gradations to it; that way you make sure you're only affecting the same colors. Use Command+Option+Shift+E, which will create a Stamp Visible layer. This will enable you to get rid of the working layers that are below it, and this is actually a good trick to remember for after you've done your acne healing, but prior to your skin smoothing. Add a layer mask to your Stamp Visible layer. This will hide all of the smoothing that you've done, and now you'll just use the brush tool to bring the fixes back in, or, in other words, hide the parts you don't want.

Chapter 3
Using the Liquify Tool for More Advanced Editing + Other Techniques

As a disclaimer, I would like to state that as a general rule, I do not approve of total body reshaping unless it is used in conceptual art to make some kind of statement. While I feel that it's totally acceptable to use in order to do slight reshaping or to allow for more symmetry in a body shape, if your model is completely unrecognizable by the end of your process, you probably should ask yourself why it was necessary to make him or her look so different in the first place.

That said, let's talk about the liquefy tool. Liquify basically uses a lot of pushing, pulling and distortion of pixels to create a new shape. The tools to be found in the liquify dialog are: the forward warp tool, the reconstruct tool, the pucker tool, the bloat tool, the push left tool, the hand tool and the zoom tool. Be sure that as you work, you're zoomed into the area that you're focused on. You can always zoom out to do larger general fixes later.

Start with the pucker tool, or a combination of the pucker tool and the push left tool to start moving pixels where you want them to go. My suggestion would be to try and work on one area of the body at a time, while still keeping an eye on the picture as a whole. The last thing you want is for your upper body look great only to have the lower body look completely disproportionate. It's also important to pay attention to whether or not you're accidentally affecting parts of the image that you don't want to. This can happen if your brush is too big, or if you're having difficulty controlling your movements with only a mouse.

The freeze mask tool and thaw mask tool, which are located in the advanced tab of liquify, will help with this issue. These tools make sure that your image is protected while you adjust other parts in liquify, and then gives you the capability to remove that protection when you're finished.

The best thing about liquify, is that you can save what is called a mesh. A mesh contains all the information for all the fixes that you've done on an image. If you decide you're done for the day, you can save your mesh and then load it later when you're ready to work on that image again.

Switch back and forth between tools as needed, and be patient. As I said before, it's going to involve a lot of consciousness on your part of what size brush you need, what tool is working, and moving pixels back and forth and from side to side to get things just perfect.

Chapter 4
Colorization

People are often asking me and my other photographer friends if we can make their black and white image color. While the answer is actually yes, it doesn't really work in quite the way they might think. While you can take a color image and convert it to black and white with the click of a button or two, with black and white to color, the process is a bit more intensive.

Firstly, if you're working with an older vintage photo that might have some rips, tears or stains, you have to clean that up. Do a quick removal of any dust spots or errors before you begin.

To actually begin the colorization process, you'll need to select the object that you would like to add color to. You can do this by using any selection tool, and while I still prefer the Quick Selection tool, some people prefer the Magnetic Lasso. Go to Image>Adjustments>Hue/Saturation, and play around until you get the color you want in your selection. If it appears that at first nothing is happening in your image, just make sure that you have the colorize checkbox checked. Once you're satisfied, click OK and move to the next part. If you find that your image is too flat (or colorized looking) for your taste, you can add in some noise, or the effect of film grain by accessing it in the filter gallery. Play around not only with the noise filter but with the grain filter as well until you get the effect you like. Basically, you are going to repeat this process with all the parts you want to colorize until you're finished. After the process is complete, you may have to do some overall brightening or correction using a combination of levels, curves, and maybe even a color balance adjustment layer. Keep in mind, though, that as beautiful as a colorized image may be, it's never going to look exactly like an image that was taken in color. You can, however, add light gradations by filters on top of your hue/saturation selections.

Chapter 5
Color Enhancement

Color enhancement is basically just retouching for color, and it also involves your quality of light as well. There are many ways you can go about adjusting your color, and they don't involve defaulting to the vibrancy and saturation sliders. In fact, this is one of the worst mistakes that beginners often make. They think their colors look lackluster or off, and rather than considering what the problem is; whether it's exposure, shadows and highlights, or a weird color cast—they just crank up the saturation and call it a day. What I want to talk about in this chapter is the usage of curves and levels, and a method for pumping up color that uses the LAB channel in the Mode dropdown menu.

Firstly, for a quick fix, I would suggest working in two steps. Make a levels ad-justment level first, because in order to make sure your color is done right, you need to make sure it was taken in the right lighting. There are all sorts of default settings to choose from, available right at the top of the panel. While you can scroll through these and use them as starting points for determining where you want to go with your image, I wouldn't suggest stopping there. This is especially important because, no matter where you want to go creatively with your image, you have to have a good, properly lit and color balanced image to work from, otherwise everything gets thrown off.

So, before you move a slider, consider what is wrong with your image. Does it have any severe, blown out highlights or unwanted shadows? If so, that's where you need to begin. Moving the darks slider to the right is going to darken your overall image, the grey slider moves the midtones up and down, and moving the lights slider to the left will lighten the image. Use the provided histogram as a guide; it will show you where the valleys and peaks of your lights and darks in the image are. The excellent thing about working on an adjustment layer as opposed to just accessing levels from the dropdown menu is that you can apply layer masks as necessary, so that you only put light corrections where you want them. This is great for situations where you may have a well-exposed image except for in one pesky spot. With the adjustment layer, you can leave the majority of the image as it is and change the things you need to.

Curves are a little bit more complicated, but they operate under the same principle. You will see a histogram that represents the light patterns in your image, along with a moveable line graph. You can move this by hand to affect your changes, or you can use the highlight, midtone, and shadow eyedropper tools to click directly onto the image and affect it that way.

Once you're satisfied with all your lighting changes, it's time to look at colors. You're going to create a color balance adjustment layer, and then take a good look at your image. As you can see, the dialog box has a set of three sliders, cyan and red, magenta and green, and yellow and blue. Adjust these sliders as needed and pay attention to whether you have highlights, shadows, or midtones selected in the dropdown menu at the top. You'll have to make minute corrections every time you make a change, and make sure the three elements look color balanced to normal. In order to ensure that you won't have any other weird color shifts on printing or posting online, you should make sure your monitor is calibrated properly. Once you've got your normal color balance, then you can concern yourself with things like whether or not the colors need more vibrancy, saturation, or desaturation.

Even though all this may sound like a lot of correction, it actually isn't that much, especially if you've already got a pretty good image to begin with. Remember to use the adjustment layers rather than just the dropdown menu alone for added ease if you mess up.

Let's talk about another way to get your light and color to pop. This also involves using Curves, but in conjunction with the LAB mode of color. The LAB channel is different because using it affects the lightness of the image instead of the color. Choose a flattened image, and change the mode to LAB. As always, duplicate your background layer, because this is where you're going to apply your changes. Now open curves, and again, this is one of the few instances where you DON'T want to use an adjustment layer, because the image you're working on needs to stay flattened. In this case, because the L channel controls the lightness, you won't even have to pull up a second dialog to work on color and light; it can be done all at once. After you adjust your L channel, select A, which is the magenta and green channel. Green is left and magenta is right, and you want to drag each side in the same number of squares. Repeat the same process with the B curve. Apply the curve, and then change the image mode back to RGB. Do not flatten the layer. Then, adjust the opacity on the top layer until you see the original begin to meld back in. Adjust it until the color corrections affects the picture as much as you want it to. You should also experiment with blend modes to see how they affect your fix.

Chapter 6
Background Removal

There are many ways that you can choose to do a background removal, and many reasons why you might do so. Background removal is especially good for things like product shots, where you'll want to be able to paste the image of the product into an ad layout. Typically, product shots are going to be the easiest type of background removal, because they are generally taken on a clean white or solid colored background. However, if you aren't working with a product shot, the process might be a little more difficult due to Photoshop's tools picking up unwanted color pixels. However, it can be cleaned up. Background removal is generally a quick process unless there are many tiny elements involved, (such as a large group of people or a very similar colored background behind an object—white on white is hard to separate), but it does have multiple steps.

Keep in mind that as with anything in Photoshop, you may find a method or tutorial that works better for you, and as such, I would suggest you experiment with all the tools that are useful for background removal, including Quick Selection, Magic Wand, and Lasso. However, for this method, we will be starting with a Quick Selection, which is my favorite way to start things off.

With Quick Selection, you'll want to make sure that the brush up at the top with the plus is selected. This is going to allow you to select pixels. Draw loosely with your mouse around the subject. The Quick Selection tool is going to do a pretty good job, but it might miss some tiny sections or details that you'll need to zoom in and make sure to select. If the brush selects too many pixels, you'll want to adjust your brush size, and also select the minus brush, which is going to allow you to deselect pixels. It works exactly the same way, just brush it over the area you'd like to remove. Again, you might have to zoom in and out to make sure it's good, but don't worry about getting it too perfect just yet.

Up at the top along with the brushes is a checkbox labeled "Refine Edges". Once you feel your selection is fairly good, click this box and another dialog box will appear. Your selection will appear isolated on a white ground, and this way you can check to see how clean your edges truly are. I would suggest checking the box labeled Smart Radius to use as a starting point, and using the sliders to refine further from there. You can also erase or add to the selection that you see by using the brush and eraser tools that will appear in the upper left hand corner. Also try the Refine Radius checkbox. I understand that this one can be a bit confusing, simply because when you first click it, Photoshop gives you a white plane with nothing on it. But, if you notice, in the section under Edge Detection, your radius is controlled by a slider and by default, and it always starts at zero. If you move the slider, you will begin to see the edges of your selection appear. You want to keep dragging until you have a pretty good outline and you can see that Photoshop is picking up all the tiny details that you want, but be sure not to push it too far. If your selection is still a bit messy, you might begin to select bits of background. A lot of these adjustments require back and forth of looking at the preview, looking at the radius, playing around with your edges and so forth. It might take a couple of tries to get your image exactly where you want it to be. When you're satisfied, click OK.

Now, you'll want to select the inverse of your image by right-clicking. Something important to note: this is not the same thing as inverting your image. When you right-click, a menu will appear. Select Inverse, and then add a layer mask. The background will disappear and your subject will be left floating on an empty layer. If you find that you still have bits of background that don't belong, simply use the minus brush to remove more. You may also want to go back into the refine edges dialog and do a final fix. If you prefer, at this point you could also choose to work directly on the layer mask by selecting your brush tool. The great thing about inverting to create a layer mask is that if you decide you want your background back, you can just chuck the layer mask.

Again, there are other ways to do this, but try this method first. I would also add that if you are having trouble (because of color similarities) of unwanted subject pixels getting picked up, try switching over to the Magic Wand tool before you finish. With the Magic Wand, you can set your tolerance and your sample point to only pick up certain colors.

You can now copy and paste or drag your selection onto a new background if desired.

Chapter 7
Camera RAW

I can never seem to talk enough about how much I value Camera RAW. I'm not going to go through all of its functions, as that could fill another entire book, but I do want to express how important it is that you should always shoot your images as a raw file and do the vast majority of any fixes you may need in Camera Raw. The program can help you to pull a lot more out of an image than may have been possible if it was just a jpeg. As always, if you do need to save your image as a jpeg, make sure that you always save a master copy in CR2 format, so that if need be, you can go back and make any necessary changes by accessing Camera Raw via the filters menu. Even if you still prefer to do your fixes in regular old Photoshop, at least do your exposure and white balance adjustments in Camera Raw, as it will make everything else that much easier to work with.

As you learn the program, you may find that you like it even more than Pho-toshop, and may reserve Photoshop for fixes that can only be done in the filters gallery.

Chapter 8
HDR

HDR is one of those things that looks really complicated but isn't actually that hard to do. To start with, you are going to need at least. The way HDR works is to utilize different exposures in order to be combined and give you the most information in the image as is possible. HDR stands for: High Dynamic Range imaging. That's what makes the image looks so sharp and clear, and in some cases almost surreal. Typically, in normal images, the sensor takes an average of the scene, and so you will have some areas that fall deeply into shadow or may be underexposed. With HDR, this doesn't happen, because by combining the images, you are getting the proper exposure in each piece of the scene.

What you do is take the exposure as you normally would for your subject. Having determined that appropriate exposure, you should go both one stop above and one stop below that one. These will give you the minimum range that you need for both your shadow and highlight detail. Again, this is the minimum, and if you would like to capture even more nuance of detail I would suggest going two stops above and below your base exposure.

After you have your images, you're going to go into Photoshop, and your first impulse may be to open up all these images that you've just taken, but all you need to do is go to File>Automate>Merge to HDR Pro. When you select Merge to HDR Pro, a dialog box will open where you're going to be asked to select your files. Select all the files you took of the scene, and hit OK. Depending upon whether the image is set to 8-bit, 16-bit, or 32-bit mode, you'll have some different options for your editing. If it's set to 8-bit or 16-bit, you're going to see quite a few options. If you are a visual learner, I would suggest also searching for some guiding images to go along with these instructions.

8 and 16-bit images are going to show quite a few editing sections in the dialog box. The first is a checkbox labeled Remove Ghosts. Check this box if you see that you've got some funky blur going on, which is typically caused by camera shaking or extraneous light spillage at night. Next is your Edge Glow, which, as it sounds, controls the amount of light, or halo, that you have around your subject. You can make it effect more or less of the picture with the radius slider, and also adjust brightness. Next are your tone and detail sliders, followed by sliders and curves that control your shadows, highlights, vibrancy, and saturation, just like with any photo. Adjust these just as you would normally, until you are satisfied with the appearance of your photo.

After you're finished adjusting your image in its 8 or 16-bit state, convert the mode to 32-bit using the dropdown menu at the very top of the dialog box. When using the white point preview slider, you won't see much of a difference as you move the slider along. While HDR works best as a 32-bit file, it's hard for computer monitors to display all of this information, so the white point preview slider is really there as a visual guide. The histogram's dips and points represent where and how the information falls within the photograph.

Once all of these preliminary steps have been done, it's time to do some tone mapping, which is the step where you are really going to get the most control and creativity out of your image. If you are using Creative Cloud, as in this book, you have the option to do your tone mapping in Camera RAW. Just make sure the box is checked if you would like that option. In older versions of Photoshop, (or just based on personal preference) you can just continue to work in the HDR dialog. You want to make sure that you do all of your tone mapping with the image in 32-bit mode, but whenever you're satisfied with your image, save it as a 8-bit or 16-bit image. Just as with any editing job on a regular photo, it's going to take some playing around with your sliders in order to get your image to exactly where you'd like it to be. Also be aware that as long as you have saved a master copy of your 32-bit image, you can tone map over and over in order to create different aesthetics for the same photo.

In the main HDR dialog box, there are also presets that will give your photos different looks. While I really wouldn't suggest hitting a preset and being done with it, you can definitely use it as a starting point or to see what your aesthetic preference might be. My own personal tips for HDR would are that you want to use it as a tool for enhancement of an already beautiful photo. The point of HDR is to make things look more real, and while pushing the boundary into hyperrealism can be kind of cool, you don't want to overdo it or it will look incredibly obvious.

Alternative to doing actual HDR, you can do something called HDR toning. This can be done with any normal PNG, JPEG or other file that you've shot, and you only need one. To open the dialog box, go to Image>Adjustments>HDR Toning, and when you click on it, the image will go to an auto HDR look, and then you can make your adjustments. Even though this isn't true HDR, the slider controls work the same and it'll do in a pinch for the aesthetic. The dialog box features the exact same sliders as actual HDR. When you're satisfied, just click OK.

No matter which route you choose, HDR is one way to experiment with Pho-toshop, have fun, and make your images stand out.

Chapter 9
What's a Smart Object? +
Smart Filters + Batch Editing

Smart objects can be created via the Layers panel by right clicking when you want to create them. A Smart Object allows you to incorporate things like vector graphics or illustration into your image plane. Transforming something into a Smart Object allows you to prevent loss of image quality. It's more digitally archival, by saving a linked copy of the information to the original image. That way, Smart objects save what you do, much in the way that layers preserve what you do. Smart objects are less archival than vectors, in that when you do any resizing, you still lose image quality, but they're definitely more archival than just working with plain pixels alone.

Smart objects also make the Free Transform tools more archival by saving all the pixels and the transformation, so that if you need to, you can return to it and make changes later on. And if you share, or copy and paste a smart object, when you make a change to one version of the image, you have the option to make the change to them all, thus expediting any work you may have to do. Smart objects can also be linked, can be shared via copy, and include nondestructive Smart Filters, which can be stacked together and then edited individually. I have never had much cause to use a Smart Object in the past, but given the advent of Smart Filters as well I may have to do more research into them and give them a try.

The last thing I wanted to mention is what is called batch editing. Batch editing is exactly as it sounds and allows you to make changes to many images at once. To create a batch, you will go to

Window>Action and you'll create a new batch by clicking on the folder icon at the top of the dropdown menu that pops up. Name your batch in the folder and then name the action below that. Make it descriptive, and relating to whatever fix you're going to have to do.

What Photoshop does is records whatever action you do on the screen as part of that action batch. This way, you only have to perform all of the actions on one photo. Press stop action when you're done. Subsequently, you will be able to load that action and apply it to the batch.

To apply the action, go to File>Automate>Batch. Select the action, set the source, and set the batch destination to none. Hit OK, and Photoshop will per-form your batch edits for you, which should help save on time with like edits from the same shoot or series.

Conclusion

As you hopefully learned from this article, there are a multitude of things that can be done in Photoshop, and tons of ways to do them. In fact, given that you are using the appropriate tools for the job and a nondestructive workflow, there are likely many ways to do the same tasks as described above. In conjunction to this book, I would also suggest doing research into the types of fixes that you use the most, and figuring out what workflow and combination of tools is the most beneficial to you.

Always keep in mind the importance of layers for preserving a master image as well as tracking all of the changes that you make. Label everything, and if you're ever doing many changes on one image, put like edits into their own folders for easier organization.

Also keep in mind that though all of the fixes that have been mentioned in this book are fairly easy to grasp, they build upon each other's principles and can take some time to master. If you find yourself struggling with the fine motor movements of certain fixes, as I have in the past, it might be a good idea to invest in a larger desktop monitor as opposed to a laptop, and a Wacom or other brand of tablet to allow you to have a more natural style of control. Tablets, too, require practice to learn to use, but once you master it, it's very worthwhile and useful.

And, with every new edition of Photoshop, be sure that you brush up on what changes and fixes have been done, as Adobe is constantly working to improve the user friendliness of their products.

Did you Like "Photoshop 2"?

Before you go, I'd like to say thank you so much for purchasing my book.

I know you could have picked from dozens of books on this subject, but you took a chance with mine, and I'm truly grateful for that.

So, once again, a big thanks for downloading this book and reading all the way to the end—I truly appreciate it.

Now I'd like to ask for a small favor if you don't mind:

Would you be so kind as to take a minute of your time and leave a review for this book on Amazon?

This feedback will help me continue to write the kind of books that help you get results. And if you loved it, then please feel free to let me know! :)

More Books by James Carren

Portrait Photography - 9 Tips Your Camera Manual Never Told You About Portrait Photography

Landscape Photography - 10 Essential Tips to Take Your Landscape Photography to The Next Level

Photography Lighting - Top 10 Must-Know Photography Lighting Facts to Shoot Like a Pro in Your Home Studio

Photography For Beginners - From Beginner To Expert Photographer In Less Than a Day!

Photography Business: 20 Things You Need to Know Before Starting a Successful Photography Business